FLANNEL HUNTING CAMP COOKBOOK

Second Edition

By Tim Murphy

For more titles in "Flannel John's Cookbooks for Guys" series, visit www.flanneljohn.com

FLANNEL JOHN'S HUNTING & FISHING CAMP COOKBOOK
Second Edition

Table of Contents

FLANNEL JOHN'S HUNTING & FISHING CAMP COOKBOOK

There is more to camp cooking than just the "Three B's" - Beans, Beef Jerky and Budweiser. Because you're in the woods and wild doesn't mean you have to act like an animal. There is nothing better than a hot, rib-sticking meal to kick-start a morning or wrap-up a day. It takes the chill out of your bones and fans the flame of hope for the next day. So for all of you who spend hours in a duck blind, deer stand, ice shanty or fishing boat, this food is for you. These recipes have been gathered from family and friends, cooks and chefs, farmers and hunters, anglers and eaters. It's camp comfort food that's simple, straightforward and for the most part, simple to prepare. Even novice camp cooks should be able to master these recipes. Still, always keep a fire extinguisher nearby if only for the chili recipes. As for the "Three B's" you will still use them as ingredients. Time to fire up the stove, heat up the grill and rummage through the pantry! It's time to ring that dinner bell!

BREAKFAST

BELGIAN POPPED WAFFLES

2 cups of biscuit mix
1 egg
3 tablespoons oil
1 1/4 cups of lemon-lime or club soda

Mix thoroughly. Pour into a pre-heated waffle iron or on griddle for pancake-style. Makes a half-dozen. Experiment with different carbonated beverages. Cherry Coke turned out pretty good.

BREAKFAST BACON PIE

12 slices of bacon, fried and crumbled
4 eggs
2 cups of milk
1 cup shredded cheese, Swiss or cheddar
¼ cup of chopped onion
1 cup of Bisquick
¼ teaspoon of pepper
¼ teaspoon salt

Lightly grease pie plate. Sprinkle bacon, cheese and onion in pie plate. Beat remaining ingredients until smooth. Pour evenly into pie plate. Bake at 400 degrees for 35 minutes. Let stand for 5 minutes before cutting.

BREAKFAST SHAKE

2 scoops of low fat yogurt
½ banana
½ cup of fresh fruit of choice
1 cup of skim milk
2 ice cubes

Mix all ingredients in a blender, the battery-powered type for those non-electric camps. Or put into a jug and shake until your arms are exhausted.

BROWNED BREAKFAST HASH

2 cups of cooked, chopped beef, chicken or
   ham
2 cups of cooked potatoes, diced
1½ onions, minced
2 tablespoons of parsley
1 cup of milk
Salt and pepper
Vegetable oil or Crisco

Mix all ingredients except milk. Place oil or Crisco in a skillet over medium heat. When hot, spread has mix evenly in skillet. Brown bottom of hash quickly, 10 to 15 minutes. Now add milk and mix. Cover and cook slowly until crisp, about 10 minutes.

CINNAMON MONKEY BREAD

3 cans of refrigerated biscuits, quartered
1 cup of sugar
¾ cup of butter
2 teaspoons of cinnamon

Cook sugar, butter and cinnamon on low heat while cutting up biscuits into a non-stick Bundt pan. Pour mixture over the top and bake at 350 degrees for 30 minutes. Cover for first 10 minutes of baking with tin foil.

EGG CASSEROLE

8 eggs
2 cups of milk
1 teaspoon of salt
7 slices of bread, cubed
1 cup of grated cheddar cheese
1 pound of ham, sausage or bacon,
  cooked and shredded

Beat eggs well and mix with milk and salt. Stir in cubed bread and grated cheese. Cut or shred meat into small pieces and add them to mixture. Pour into a greased 8 x 10 inch dish and bake at 350 degrees for 45 minutes.

EGGNOG WAFFLES

2 cups of biscuit mix (Bisquick)
¼ teaspoon of nutmeg
1½ cups of eggnog
2 tablespoons of salad oil
1 egg

Mix all ingredients thoroughly until smooth. A rotary mixer may be helpful. Pour into waffle maker or onto a griddle for a pancake-style.

HAM & EGG SCRAMBLE

1 package of frozen fried potatoes
2 cups of ham, cubed
4 eggs
1 small onion, diced
Butter or margarine
Salt, pepper or seasoning to taste

Fry potatoes in butter and add diced or chopped onion. Beat eggs and pour over potato mixture. After eggs are pretty well cooked, add ham and cook on low for 15 minutes.

HUEVOS RANCHEROS

2 tablespoons of cooking oil
1 small green or red pepper, finely chopped
1 small onion, chopped
1 clove of garlic, minced (optional)
1 teaspoon of chili powder
8 ounces of tomato sauce
1 pound of tomatoes, chopped
6 eggs
1 package of tortillas (fried flour, chips, etc)
Salt and pepper

Heat cooking oil in a large skillet and sauté pepper, onion and garlic until mushy. Stir in chili powder, tomato sauce and tomatoes. Cook until bubbly. Lower heat and season with salt and pepper to taste. Drops eggs into hot sauce and simmer over low heat, covered, until eggs are firm. Serve eggs with tomato sauce and tortillas.

POTATO PANCAKES

4 cups of mashed potatoes
1 tablespoon of flour

Mix potatoes and flour. Divide in half. On a floured surface, roll out each half to ¼-inch thickness. Cut mixture with round cookie cutter (can with lid and bottom removed). Place in a medium-hot skillet and fry on un-greased pan until brown on both sides.

ROOKIE COOK FRENCH TOAST

2 cups of milk
4 eggs
½ teaspoon salt
2 teaspoons of cinnamon
Sliced bread
Oil

Beat four eggs thoroughly then mix all ingredients together. Dip bread into mixture until well coated. Fry on an oiled griddle or skillet until golden brown.

SPAM, EGGS & RICE

12 ounces of Spam (1 can)
3 cups of rice, cooked
8 eggs
Soy sauce

Cut Spam into ¼-inch slices. Brown both sides in skillet and set aside. Cook rice and set aside. Scramble 8 eggs in skillet. Put rice on plates, top with eggs and put Spam on the side. Sprinkle with soy sauce.

SUNRISE WAFFLES

   1 cup of flour
   2 eggs
   4 tablespoons of melted butter
   2 teaspoons of baking powder
   1 cup of milk

Beat egg yolks and add milk, butter and flour. Mix thoroughly. Add egg whites. This will fill the iron 3 or 4 times

CHILI, SOUP & STEW

A LONG DAY'S STEW

12 small red potatoes
1 head of green cabbage chopped in chunks
1½ onions, diced
2 quarts of water
1 cup of carrots, diced
1 cup of celery, diced
2 pounds kielbasa, Polish or smoked sausage

Heat water; add onions, potatoes and cabbage. Cut sausage into pieces and add into pot along with potatoes. Bring to a boil. Cook until onions and potatoes are soft enough to eat. Bold eaters can add Tabasco, garlic or pepper to taste

BASIC CHILI

1 pound of ground beef, seasoned to taste
1 onion, diced
1 cup of celery, diced
2 cans of kidney or chili beans (drained)
48 ounces of tomato juice
1 teaspoon of chili powder (optional)
Hot sauce to taste

Brown onion and hamburger in a skillet then drain grease. Combine all ingredients in a Dutch oven or large kettle; simmer for 60 to 75 minutes. For white chili, substitute ground beef with ground turkey or shredded chicken.

BASIC CHILI II – THE REVENGE!

1 pound of ground beef
½ onion, diced
1 green pepper, chopped
1 package of chili seasoning
1 large can of small red beans, drained
1 large can of chili beans
1 medium can of whole tomatoes, diced
Salt, pepper and cumin to taste

Brown the ground beef then add chopped onion and green pepper. Drain the grease. Add chili seasoning, red beans, chili beans and tomatoes and stir. When mixture begins to boil, turn the heat to low and cook for 2 hours covered.

CHICKEN & RICE SOUP

6 cups of chicken broth
1 cup of rice
3 eggs, separated
Juice from 1 lemon
Salt and pepper

Boil 6 cups of broth, add one cup of rice. Salt and pepper to taste. When rice is cooked, lower heat to a simmer. In a bowl, beat 3 egg whites until stiff. Slowly add yokes and juice from lemon. Beat well. Add broth a ladle at a time beating well into most of the broth is used. Pour mixture back into pot, stirring well. Chicken may be added to soup.

CHEDDAR CHEESE SOUP

½ cup of butter or margarine
6 tablespoons of flour
1 quart of milk
1 teaspoon of salt
2 cups of sharp cheddar cheese, shredded
½ cup of celery, diced
½ cup of green pepper, diced
½ cup of onion, diced
½ cup of carrots, diced
16 ounces of chicken stock or broth

Combine flour, milk, cheese and salt and make a thick sauce. Sauté` celery, green peppers, onions and carrots in butter. Add chicken broth and cook until hot and vegetables are crunchy, then add to cheese sauce. Stir thoroughly.

DEER TAG STEW

2 pounds of venison, cut into pieces
2 large onions, diced
3 carrots, diced large
1 small can of corn
1 clove of garlic, minced
4 medium potatoes, cubed
24 ounces of tomato sauce
1 tablespoon of salt
1 tablespoon of celery salt
2 tablespoons of black pepper

Combine all ingredients in a large pot on low heat for 35 to 45 minutes. Once ingredients are tender, remove lid and simmer until thick. Serve hot with corn bread.

FRENCH ONION SOUP

4 large onions, thinly sliced
4 tablespoons of margarine
10 ounces of beef broth
½ cup of dry sherry
2 teaspoons of Worcestershire sauce
Pinch of pepper
French Bread, thinly sliced
6 slices of Swiss cheese
Parmesan cheese

Brown onion in margarine until tender. Add in beef broth, sherry, Worcestershire and pepper. Bring to a boil. In six individual bowls, pour the soup, float bread with slice of Swiss cheese on top. Sprinkle with Parmesan. Bake at 375 degrees for 15 to 20 minutes or under a broiler for 5 minutes.

IRISH STEW

2 pounds of ground beef, turkey or venison
1 can of corn
1 can of peas
1 cup of celery, diced
1 cup of onion, diced
1 cup of carrots, diced
3 cups of potatoes, diced
1 can of whole tomatoes
1 tablespoon of salt
Pepper to taste

Brown hamburger and onions in a skillet. Add remaining ingredients and cook on low heat for about two hours. Stir occasionally.

JERKY CHILI

½ cup of chopped bacon
1 onion, diced
2 cloves of garlic, minced
2 cups of beef broth
4 chili peppers, chopped
2 tablespoons of chili powder
2 tablespoons of light brown sugar
1½ tablespoons of cumin
5 cups of fresh tomatoes, peeled and chopped
½ tablespoon of pepper
2½ cups of beef or buffalo jerky, chopped
2½ cups kidney or pinto beans, cooked

Cook bacon in deep pot or Dutch oven until fat is released, but not crisp. Add onion and garlic and cook until tender. Add in chili peppers, tomatoes and broth. Cook until tomatoes are soft, 15 to 20 minutes. Now combine chili powder, brown sugar, cumin and pepper and then add to pot. Stir in the beef jerky. Simmer or low boil for 45 minutes. Add beans and boil for about 5 minutes.

MINERS' STEW

This recipe was inspired by recipes from the mining towns in northern Minnesota and Michigan's Upper Peninsula. The taste is as rich as the history.

1 pound of ground beef
2 celery stalks, diced
3 potatoes, chopped
1 large carrot, diced
1 large can of tomato soup
1 small onion, diced
½ teaspoon of salt
½ teaspoon of pepper
¼ teaspoon of basil
¼ teaspoon of rosemary
¼ teaspoon of sage
1 tablespoon of flour mixed with 2
    tablespoons of water

Cook ground beef and onion in a skillet. Drain. In a large stew pan or pot, add beef, onion, tomato soup and 2 cans of water. Mix well. Add remaining ingredients. Cook on medium low heat until carrots and potatoes soften. Add flour paste to thicken and stir.

PUMPKIN SOUP

1 stick of butter
1 onion, coarsely chopped
5 pounds of pumpkin
1 cup of heavy cream
1 quart of water
1 pinch of nutmeg
Salt and pepper

Wash and peel pumpkin and remove seeds. Cut pumpkin into 2-inch cubes. Melt butter in large pot and add onions. Cook onions until tender. Add pumpkin and water. Season with salt, pepper and nutmeg. Simmer for 20 to 30 minutes. Puree mixture and add cream. If too thick add water.

VENISON CHILI

2 pounds of ground venison
¼ cup of cooking oil
1 cup of onion, diced
2 cloves of garlic, minced
1 large green pepper, chopped
3 tablespoons of chili powder
2 cups of tomatoes
1 cup of tomato sauce
1 cup of water
½ teaspoon salt
3 cups of kidney beans, cooked
1 tablespoon of flour mixed with 2
   tablespoons of water

Brown venison in oil in a deep pot or Dutch oven until meat loses pink color. Add onion, garlic and green pepper and cook for an additional 5 minutes. Stir in chili powder, tomatoes, tomato sauce, water and salt. Simmer for 2 hours. Add flour paste and cook until mixture thickens. Stir in kidney beans and cook for another 15 minutes.

WHITE CHILI

1 tablespoon of olive oil

4 chicken breast halves, boneless, skinless and cubed

1 cup of onion, diced

1 tablespoon of garlic, minced

8 ounces of canned green chilies, chopped

2 tablespoons of ground cumin

1½ teaspoons of dried oregano

¼ teaspoon of ground cloves

¼ teaspoon of ground cayenne pepper

16 ounces of chicken broth

1 teaspoon of salt

½ teaspoon of pepper

12 ounces Monterey Jack cheese, shredded

2 cans white beans, rinsed and drained

Heat olive oil over medium-high heat in deep pot or Dutch oven. Add chicken, onion and sauté until chicken is no longer pink. Stir in garlic, chilies, cumin, oregano, cloves and cayenne pepper. Sauté for 3 minutes until flavors blend. Add beans and broth and simmer for 20 minutes. Season with salt and pepper.

BURGERS & SANDWICHES

BARBECUED NOT-SO-SLOPPY JOES

1 pound of ground beef
1 cup of onion, diced
1 cup of ketchup
2 tablespoons of mustard
1 teaspoon of salt
1 teaspoon of sugar
1 teaspoon of vinegar
½ teaspoon of cloves (optional)

Brown ground beef and onions. Stir in remaining ingredients. Cover and simmer 30 minutes. Optional method: form 4 to 6 patties with all ingredients and toss them on the grill.

BARBECUE PORK BURGERS

2 pounds of ground pork
¼ cup of fresh breadcrumbs
1 cup of barbecue sauce
6 burger buns
Salt and pepper (optional)

Mix ground pork with breadcrumbs and ½ cup of sauce to make six patties. Grill burgers on medium high heat, basting burgers often with remaining sauce. Takes about ten minutes to cook, five minutes per side.

BLEU CHEESE BURGERS

2 pounds of ground beef
8 ounces of blue cheese, crumbled
2 tablespoons of onion powder
2 tablespoons of garlic powder
2 tablespoons of soy sauce
2 teaspoons of salt
4 slices of Swiss cheese
4 hamburger buns

Combine ground beef, blue cheese onion powder, garlic powder, soy sauce and salt in a bowl. Mix well to make 4 large patties. Grill patties on high heat for about 8 minutes per side or until well done. Top with Swiss cheese

GRILLED CHEESE PIZZA SANDWICH

8 slices of bread
¾ cup of pizza sauce
8 slices of mozzarella cheese
24 slices of pepperoni
2 tablespoons of Crisco
Toppings of choice

Spread 1 teaspoon of sauce on each piece of bread. Place slice of cheese on 4 bread slices and 6 slices of pepperoni. Add other four slices of cheese and bread. Melt 1 tablespoon of Crisco in skillet on medium heat and add sandwiches. Grill 2 to 4 minutes until golden brown. Add remaining Crisco, let melt and turn sandwiches to grill other side.

PORCELAIN PALACE MINI BURGERS

1½ pounds of ground beef
1 egg
1 envelope of instant onion soup mix
½ cup diced onion
2 teaspoons water

Mix and press into a cookie sheet. Poke holes in meat placing diced onions in holes. Bake at 400 degrees for 10 minutes. Cut into squares use dinner rolls for buns.

QUESADILLA BURGER

6 ounces of ground beef
2 ounces of salsa
1 ounce of cheddar cheese, shredded
1 burger bun
Hot sauce (optional)

Grill the burger and place on the bun. Top with a few drops of hot sauce, salsa and cheese.

SLOPPY JOE

1 pound of ground beef
1 package of French's Sloppy Joe mix
6 ounces of tomato paste
1 can of chicken & rice soup
1 soup can of water
1 onion, diced
1 bell pepper, diced

Brown hamburger or deer meat in a skillet. Drain the fat then add sloppy Joe mix, tomato paste, soup and water. Simmer for 30 minutes. Serve on bread or buns.

ULTIMATE GRILLED CHEESE SANDWICH

3 ounces of softened cream cheese
¾ cup of mayonnaise
1 cup of cheddar cheese, shredded
1 cup of mozzarella cheese, shredded
½ teaspoon of garlic powder
Seasoned salt to taste
10 slices of Italian bread, ½-inch thick
2 tablespoons butter

In a bowl, mix cream cheese and mayonnaise until smooth. Stir in cheese, garlic powder and seasoning salt. Spread 5 slices of bread with cheese mixture and top with remaining bread. Butter outside of sandwich and toast in a large pan or skillet for about 4 minutes a side or until golden brown.

VENISON BURGERS

1½ pounds of ground venison
4 tablespoons of red wine
3 tablespoons of breadcrumbs
6 strips of bacon
3 tablespoons of melted butter
Salt and pepper

Mix meat with wine and breadcrumbs. Refrigerate 1 to 2 hours. Shape into patties and wrap a bacon strip around each. Pin it with a toothpick. Brush patties with melted butter, salt and pepper to taste. Grill, basting with butter.

MAIN DISHES

ALOHA CHICKEN

2 pounds of chicken pieces
¾ cup of sugar
2 eggs, beaten
1 cup of flour
1½ cups of ketchup
¼ cup of pineapple, crushed
½ cup of vinegar
1 teaspoon of salt
1 teaspoon of soy sauce
Garlic salt to taste

Wash and drain chicken. Lightly sprinkle with garlic salt. Let stand 5 to 10 minutes. Dip chicken in beaten eggs then coat with flour. Fry until browned then put in a baking pan. In a saucepan combine remaining ingredients and bring to a boil. Pour over chicken and bake at 350 degrees for 50 minutes. Serve with rice pouring any extra sauce over the rice.

AVOCADO STEAK

1 sirloin steak (or tenderized venison steak)
¼ cup of horseradish sauce, mild or strong
1 avocado, sliced

Place steak on a broiler pan and cook about 6 inches from the heat until it reaches desired doneness. Then spread horseradish sauce on both sides of the steak and top with avocado slices. Broil for 2 more minutes.

BAKED FISH

12 cleaned pan fish (fresh or frozen)
¼ cup of butter or margarine
1 can of cream of celery soup
½ cup of lemon juice
¼ cup parsley flakes

Melt butter in 9-inch by 13-inch pan. Arrange fish in butter. Pour other ingredients, one at a time, over fish. Bake at 350 degrees for 50 minutes or until fish flakes easily.

BARBECUED FISH

4 fish fillets
1 tablespoon of oil
Barbecue sauce
½ onion, diced
4 strips of bacon, cooked & crumbled or
   bacon bits
Lemon pepper seasoning

Spread cooking oil in aluminum foil. Place fish fillets in foil and sprinkle with lemon pepper seasoning. Cover fillets with onion and bacon bits then cover with sauce. Place on grill or in oven at 350 degrees. Cook until fish is white and flaky. Dense fish like salmon may require higher heat and longer cooking time.

BARBECUED BEEF (OR VENISON)

4 pound beef roast (or venison)
1 cup of ketchup
1 cup of barbecue sauce
2 cups of celery, diced
2 tablespoons of vinegar
2 tablespoons of brown sugar
2 tablespoons of Worcestershire sauce
1 teaspoon of chili powder
1 teaspoon of garlic powder
1 teaspoon of salt

Place roast in a baking dish. Mix all ingredients into a sauce and pour over the meat. Bake at 300 degrees for 4 to 5 hours. Shred beef or venison with fork and serve on rolls, buns or bread.

BEEF & RICE CASSEROLE

1 pound of ground beef
2 cans of cream of onion soup
1 envelope of dry onion soup mix
1 cup of uncooked rice

Mix all ingredients and bake in a covered dish at 350 degrees for 60 minutes.

BEEF STEW & DUMPLINGS

24 ounces of canned beef stew
1 can of tomato soup
1 soup can water
1 cup Bisquick
¼ cup water

In a saucepan combine stew, soup and water. Bring to a boil. Mix Bisquick and ¼ cup of water and drop by spoonfuls into boiling stew. Cook uncovered on low heat for about 10 minutes (stove or grill). Cover and cook for 10 more minutes.

BEER BATTER FISH

6 fish fillets
2 eggs, separated
¾ cup of beer
1 cup of flour
½ teaspoon of salt
½ teaspoon of paprika (optional)
2 tablespoons melted butter, cooled

Beat egg yolks until thick, gradually mix in beer. Add salt, flour, paprika and melted butter. Stir mixture until smooth. Beat egg whites until stiff and fold into batter, mix thoroughly. Wipe fish dry before dipping in batter. Fry in pan or deep fryer.

BIG BUSTER'S BEEF DINNER

1 pound of ground beef
1 clove of garlic, minced
1 teaspoon of salt
1 onion, finely chopped
1 green pepper, finely chopped
1 teaspoon of chili pepper
2½ cups of tomatoes, diced
1 can of kidney beans
¾ cup of rice
¾ cup of grated cheese

Brown meat until it crumbles. Stir in garlic, salt, onion, green pepper and chili powder and sauté` for 5 minutes. Mix in tomatoes, beans and rice. Pour into a buttered casserole dish. Bake at 350 degrees for 45 minutes. Sprinkle with cheese and bake 15 minutes more.

BREAST OF WILD FOWL

Breast fillets of pheasant, duck or goose
Italian salad dressing
Seasoned breadcrumbs
Dijon mustard
Butter or margarine
White cooking wine

Cut fillets into thin patties. Marinate for 4 hours in salad dressing. Spread mustard on each side of fillet. Coat in seasoned breadcrumbs. Sauté` in margarine and white wine until done. Be careful not to overcook.

CAMP POTLUCK

1 chicken bouillon cube
¾ cup instant rice
1 envelope of dry onion soup mix
3 cups of water
8 ounces of soup vegetables or beans
5 ounces of chicken, diced or shredded
¼ teaspoon hot sauce (optional)

Bring water and bouillon cube to a boil. Add remaining ingredients, continuing to stir until rice is cooked.

CHEESEBURGER CHOWDER

1 pound of ground beef
4 ounces of Cheddar cheese
4 cups of milk
½ cup of celery, diced fine
¼ cup of onion, diced
2 tablespoons of green pepper, diced
3 tablespoons of flour
1 tablespoon of beef gravy base
   (bouillon can also be used)
½ teaspoon of salt

Brown beef in a pan then add celery, onion and green pepper. Cook until tender, stirring frequently. Blend in flour and salt and stir until smooth and bubbly. Stir in milk and gravy base. Simmer and stir until smooth and thick. Add cheese, simmer and stir until cheese melts.

CHICKEN & RICE CASSEROLE

2 cups of cooked rice
8 ounces of chicken, diced
1 cup crushed pineapple in its own juice
1 cup celery, thinly sliced
1 medium green pepper, diced
4 ounces cheddar cheese, shredded
4 tablespoons of mayonnaise
Salt and pepper to taste

Combine all ingredients except 2 ounces of cheese and mix well. Put in a casserole dish. Sprinkle remaining cheese over top. Bake at 350 degrees for 30 minutes.

CHICKEN FRIED VENISON

2 pounds of venison steaks
1 egg, beaten
¼ teaspoon of garlic
¼ teaspoon of onion salt
½ cup of flour
1 cup of oil
Salt and pepper

Trim fat and membrane from meat. Pound steaks to tenderize and dip each piece in egg, followed by a mixture of garlic salt, onion salt and flour. Salt and pepper to taste and fry in cooking oil.

CITRUS FISH

4 tablespoons of orange juice
4 tablespoons of soy sauce
4 tablespoons of ketchup
2 green onions, chopped
2 tablespoons of oil
1 pound of fish fillets

Mix first 5 ingredients together to make a sauce. Place the fillets in a shallow baking dish or pan and pour in half of the sauce. Broil for 8 to 12 minutes. Turn fish carefully and brush with remaining sauce. Broil until done.

CRISPY CHICKEN

1 chicken in pieces
4 cups of corn flakes
½ cup of evaporated milk
½ cup of butter
1 teaspoon of salt
Pepper to taste

Crush corn flakes into crumbs and mix with salt and pepper. Dip chicken pieces in milk and roll in seasoned crumbs. Place chicken pieces skin side up in a single layer in pan. Drizzle with melted butter. Bake at 350 degrees for 60 minutes.

DEEP FRIED PERCH

1 pound of perch, cut into 1-inch pieces
1 cup of flour
1 cup of warm beer
1 tablespoon of dry yeast
½ teaspoon of salt
24 ounces of oil (if using a deep fryer)

Mix yeast, flour and salt with ½ cup of beer and stir until smooth. Add remainder of the beer and continue to stir until smooth. Let batter stand for 30 minutes and stir batter again. Dip perch into batter and deep fry in oil at 350 degrees. If using a skillet, fry in oil on medium to high heat until golden brown.

FISH WITH DILL SAUCE

6 fish fillets
1 cup of sour cream
2 tablespoons of dill pickle juice
2 tablespoons of snipped parsley
¼ cup green pepper, chopped
1 egg
¾ cup of flour
¼ cup of butter
½ teaspoon of salt
Pinch of pepper

Beat egg and blend in 2 tablespoons of water. In a separate bowl combine flour salt and pepper. Dip fish into egg mixture coating both sides, then roll in flour mixture. Heat butter in large skillet and add single layer of fish. Fry one side until brown, turn, and fry until other side is brown. Remove fish from pan. Add in sour cream, pickle juice, parsley and green onion. Simmer until thickened. Pour this sauce over fish and serve.

FISHING CAMP STEELHEAD

4 steelhead fillets, 1-inch thick
¼ cup of oil
¼ cup of soy sauce
2 cloves of garlic, minced
3 tablespoons of parsley
Pepper to taste

Combine oil, parsley, garlic, soy sauce and pepper into a marinade. Soak the fish in the liquid for 1 o 2 hours in the fridge. Drain the marinade and save. Grill over medium-hot coals for 6 to 8 minutes flip and grill for another 6 to 8 minutes Baste fish occasionally with marinade. It can also be baked in a baking dish at 350 degrees for 18 to 22 minutes. Baste occasionally.

FOUR CORNER CHICKEN PARMESAN

3 pounds of chicken pieces
1 cup of cornflake crumbs
½ cup of Parmesan cheese, grated
¾ cup of Miracle Whip

Combine corn flake crumbs and cheese. Coat chicken pieces with the Miracle Whip and then coat with crumb and cheese mixture. Put in dish and bake at 350 degrees for 60 minutes.

GOLDEN BAKED FISH

4 fresh fish fillets
½ cup milk
1 teaspoon of salt
¾ crushed corn flakes (or Special K)
2 tablespoons of melted butter

Dissolve salt in milk. Soak fish in milk for 5 to 10 minutes than dip in crushed corn flakes. Bake on greased cookie sheet or pan at 400 degrees for 20 minutes.

HUNTERS DELIGHT

1 pound of bacon, sliced
1½ pounds of ham, cubed
1 large can tomato puree or tomato sauce
1 large can of whole kernel corn
1 can of lima beans
4 ounces of canned mushrooms, sliced
1 package of spaghetti
2 onions, sliced

Cut bacon slices in half and fry. Fry cubed ham in bacon fat. Fry sliced onion until golden brown. Cook spaghetti as to package directions. Combine all ingredients. Bake at 350 degrees for 60 to 75 minutes.

ITALIAN HALIBUT

1 pound of halibut fillets
1½ cups of spaghetti sauce
2 ounces of Parmesan cheese

Place fish in a baking dish. Pour sauce over the fish. Sprinkle Parmesan cheese over the sauce and fish. Bake at 350 degrees for 30 minutes or until fish is firm.

LASAGNA

1½ cups of water
1 large jar of spaghetti sauce
16 ounces of ricotta cheese
10 ounces of mozzarella cheese
½ cup of Parmesan cheese
½ pound of ground beef or venison
Lasagna noodles

Mix water, sauce and browned meat. Spoon a layer into a baking dish. Now cover with an overlapping layer of noodles. Next spread half the ricotta and mozzarella over noodles. Sprinkle with Parmesan and add another layer of sauce. Repeat the layers. Top with noodles and pour remaining sauce evenly and sprinkle with Parmesan. Cover with foil and place dish on a baking sheet. Bake at 350 degrees for 60 minutes. Remove foil and add a final layer of mozzarella and bake 10 minutes.

TJ'S QUICK & LAZY PIZZA

1 jar of tomato sauce
8 ounces of mozzarella cheese, shredded
1 package of pepperoni
Bagels, bread or hamburger buns

Spread sauce on your bread of choice. Top with cheese and pepperoni. Bake in pre-heated oven or toaster oven for 2 to 5 minutes. Keep an eye on it or you'll need the fire extinguisher.

MARINATED FISH

1½ pounds of fish filets
1 tomato, diced
1 red onion, diced
4 tablespoons of dill
½ teaspoon of salt
½ teaspoon of pepper

Puree all ingredients in a blender except the fish. Pour mixture over fish and marinate in refrigerator overnight. Wipe off marinade. Place fish in a skillet with a little oil and fry 4 to 8 minutes per side or until golden.

MEAT LOAF
(The food, not the singer)

2 pounds of ground beef (or venison)
1 pound of ground pork
2 cups of tomatoes, chopped
2 eggs
1 cup of sweet cream
¼ onion, minced
Salt and pepper to taste

Mix thoroughly and put mixture into a loaf pan. Bake at 350 degrees for 90 minutes.

MEAT LOAF II – THE SEQUEL

2 pounds of lean ground beef
2 cups of dry bread cubes or croutons
2 eggs
1 cup of milk
½ cup of onion, minced
1 teaspoon of Italian seasoning
1 tablespoon of garlic, minced
1 tablespoon of Worcestershire sauce
1 tablespoon of steak sauce

Combine all ingredients in a large bowl. Put mixture in a loaf pan and bake at 350 degrees for 80 to 90 minutes.

MEAT LOAF III:
RETURN OF THE MUSHROOMS

1½ pounds of ground beef
4½ tablespoons of soy sauce
1 egg
1 can of cream of mushroom soup
½ cup ketchup
¼ cup of onion, diced
¾ cup of breadcrumbs
¼ teaspoon of garlic powder
¼ teaspoon of pepper

Mix 1½ teaspoons soy sauce with ketchup and ½ can of mushroom soup. This makes the sauce. Mix remaining ingredients together and press into a greased loaf pan. Pour sauce over the loaf. Bake at 350 degrees for 45 minutes.

MEXICAN CORN BREAD BAKE

1½ pounds of ground beef
1 package of taco seasoning
½ cup of water
12 ounces of canned of corn, drained
2 packages of corn muffin mix
½ cup of green pepper, chopped
8 ounces of tomato sauce
1 can of French fried onions
¼ cup of cheese, grated

Brown the meat in a skillet and drain. Add taco seasoning, water, corn, green pepper and tomato sauce and simmer for a few minutes. Put in an 8-inch baking dish. Make muffin mix according to instructions on package. Add ½ cup of onions. Top mixture in pan with the muffin mixture. Bake at 350 degrees for 20 minutes uncovered. Remove and add cheese and remainder of canned onions. Bake for 3 more minutes.

NO-FRILLS CHICKEN

1 whole chicken, 4 pounds or more
1 heavy pot
  (Enameled cast iron works best)

Rinse but do not season or salt chicken. Place in a covered pot. Cook at 500 degrees for 45 to 50 minutes. Remove and let cool for 10 minutes. Cut into pieces or remove from bone for sandwiches, salads and soups.

PAN FRIED SMELT

2 pounds of smelt, cleaned
½ cup of cornmeal
½ cup of flour
1 tablespoon of salt
½ teaspoon of pepper
Oil

Mix cornmeal, flour, salt and pepper. Dip smelt in water and then in the cornmeal mixture. In a skillet, fry the fish in hot oil (or butter or margarine) for 4 to 5 minutes per side until golden brown.

PORK & APPLESAUCE MEAT LOAF

1½ pounds of ground beef
½ pound of ground pork
1 cup of applesauce
4 ounces of diced onion
1 cup of breadcrumbs
1 egg, lightly beaten
3 tablespoons of ketchup
2 teaspoons of salt
¼ teaspoon of pepper

Mix ingredients thoroughly and press into a loaf pan. Bake at 350 degrees for 2 hours.

ROUND STEAK WITH GRAVY

2½ pounds of round steak
1 envelope of dry onion soup mix
¼ cup water
1 can of cream of mushroom soup

Cut steak into 5 to 6 pieces. Place in a large pot or slow cooker. Add dry on onion soup mix, water and condensed mushroom soup. Cover and cook on low 6 to 8 hours.

SOUTHERN STYLE FRIED CHICKEN

2 chickens (cut into 8 pieces each)
2 cups of flour
1 cup of milk
1 teaspoon of salt
½ teaspoon of ground pepper
½ cup of butter
2 eggs

Mix milk, salt, pepper and well-beaten eggs in a bowl. Melt butter in skillet over high heat. Dip chicken pieces into milk mixture, coat with flour until completely dry and place in skillet. Turn continually until pieces are golden brown.

TACOS FROM SCRATCH

1 pound of ground beef
1 large onion, diced
1 can of kidney beans
16 bounces of tomato sauce
1 tablespoon of chili powder
1 package of taco seasoning (optional)
Taco shells
Salt and pepper
Lettuce, diced tomatoes, grated cheese,
olives and sour cream for toppings

Brown ground beef and add chopped onion. Drain kidney beans, mash and add to meat and chopped onion. Add tomato sauce, chili powder, salt and pepper. Cook until thick. Spoon into shells and add toppings.

TATER TOT HOT DISH

A nod to my bird hunting and ice-fishing brethren in Da Dakotas and Minnesota. It ain't a camp without da hot dish!

> 2 pounds of ground beef
>   (buffalo or turkey optional)
> ½ cup of onion, diced
> 2 cans of cream of mushroom soup
> 1 can of corn
> 1 bag of tater tots

Brown meat lightly and spread evenly in a 9-inch by 13-inch pan or baking dish. Cover with cream of mushroom, followed by corn and then a final layer of tater tots. Bake at 350 degrees for 30 minutes.

TERIYAKI SALMON

2 cups of soy sauce
1½ cups of cooking sherry
2 teaspoons of ginger
1 cup of brown sugar
1¼ cups of sugar
½ teaspoon of garlic powder
½ teaspoon of onion powder
1 salmon filet (halibut works too)

Mix ingredients in saucepan. Simmer on low heat for 45 minutes. Make sure sugar is completely dissolved. Let cool. Filet salmon and cut into strips crosswise. Marinate in teriyaki sauce for 1 hour. Grill to taste. If you're working with lighter tasting fish, you can use this recipe and also substitute white wine for the sherry.

TEXAS GOULASH

2 pounds of ground beef
1 can of tomatoes
2 cups of uncooked macaroni or small pasta
½ envelope of chili mix
1 onion, diced
1 can of whole kernel corn
20 ounces of beef broth or bouillon
1 tablespoon of sugar
½ cup cheese, grated (optional)
Salt, pepper, garlic and oregano to taste

Brown ground beef and onion. Add remaining ingredients and mix well. Place in crock-pot on a low setting for 3½ hours. Add cheese when goulash is done.

TOMATO COD CASSEROLE

1 pound of cod fillets
1 can of whole tomatoes
2 tablespoons of onion, finely minced
1 tablespoon of sugar
1 tablespoon of butter, melted
1 teaspoon of parsley, chopped
½ teaspoon of salt
¼ teaspoon of pepper (adjust to taste)

Pour tomatoes in a baking dish then sprinkle with onions, salt, pepper and sugar. Place fish on top of the tomatoes and sprinkle with parsley. Cover and bake at 350 degrees for 20 to 25 minutes. Sprinkle with melted butter and serve.

TUNA NOODLE CASSEROLE

1 can of peas
1 can of tuna fish
1 can of cream of mushroom soup
¼ cup of celery, diced
8 ounces of noodles
1 cup of cheddar cheese, shredded (optional)
Butter
Salt and pepper

Cook noodles in boiling, salted water. Mix ingredients. Put in a medium buttered casserole dish. Bake at 350 degrees for 30 to 40 minutes or until lightly brown.

SNACKS, SIDES
and SAUCES

BARBECUE PARTY SAUSAGE

1 pound of smoked Polish sausage
1 can of whole mushrooms
½ bottle of barbecue sauce

Bake and drain sausage and cut into bite-size chunks. Combine all ingredients, warm and serve.

BELLY UP TO THE BAR CHEESE

2 pounds of Velveeta
7 ounces of horseradish
8 drops of Tabasco sauce
1 cup of mayonnaise

Combine cheese, Tabasco and horseradish in a double boiler and melt. Do not use direct flame. Remove from the heat and stir in the mayonnaise. Pour into container and cool.

BEER BATTER FOR FISH & SHRIMP

    1 can of beer
    1 cup of flour
    1 teaspoon of salt
    2 eggs
    1 teaspoon of baking powder

Make paste with beer and flour. Add eggs, baking powder and salt. Dry fish thoroughly, dip in batter and fry at 360 degrees until golden brown

BEER CHEESE BALL

10 ounces of sharp cheddar cheese
8 ounces of softened cream cheese
½ can of beer
Garlic salt to taste

Shred the cheddar cheese. Mix all ingredients until smooth. Shape into a ball and refrigerate.

BLAZING SADDLE BAKED BEANS

5 slices of bacon, shredded
1 large onion, diced
1 large can of baked beans
¼ cup of brown sugar
½ cup of ketchup

In a skillet, cook bacon and onion until onion is soft and meat is mostly cooked without being crisp. Drain the grease. Mix all ingredients thoroughly in a baking dish. Bake mixture at 350 degrees for 60 minutes.

C.C. CHICKEN WINGS

2 pounds of chicken wings
12 ounces of cola (or cherry cola)
1 cup of ketchup
1 tablespoon of Worcestershire (optional)

Place wings in a pan. Mix the ingredients thoroughly and pour over wings. Cook at 375 degrees for 60 minutes while occasionally stirring to keep wings glazed.

CHILI CHEESEDIP

1 green pepper, chopped
1 onion, diced
2 tablespoons of butter
15 ounces of no-beans chili (canned)
1 can of cream of mushroom soup
¼ teaspoon of garlic powder
1 pound of sharp cheddar cheese, grated
Corn chips

In a skillet, sauté pepper and onion. Use a little butter if needed. Add no-beans chili, soup and garlic then simmer. Add cheese before serving. Makes a great hot dog topping too.

CHILI CON QUESO DIP

2 tablespoons of butter
16 ounces of tomato sauce
1½ pounds sharp cheddar cheese, grated
1 onion, finely chopped
8 ounces of canned green chilies seeded and
  chopped

Sauté onion in butter. Add tomato sauce or tomatoes and chilies the simmer for 10 minutes. Add grated cheese and heat until melted. Makes three cups.

CLASSIC BAKED BEANS

2 cans of pork and beans
1½ cups of brown sugar
½ cup butter
¼ teaspoon hickory seasoning
   (liquid smoke)

Drain beans and remove pork lard. Mix ingredients in bowl, place in a baking dish and bake at 250 degrees for 3 hours.

COLE SLAW SALAD

1 purple cabbage, shred fine
1 green cabbage, shred fine
1 cup of cheese, shredded
1 cup of bologna, diced (ring bologna works)
1 red onion, cut in rings
1 green pepper
Salt, pepper and garlic salt (optional)
French dressing (optional)

Finely cut cabbages, cheese, bologna onion and pepper. Toss in tomato as an option. Add seasonings to taste. Once these are all tossed together, refrigerate at least 8 hours and serve cold with dressing of choice.

CRAB DIP

1 can of crab
8 ounces of softened cream cheese
¼ pint of sour cream
¼ cup of white wine
Lowry's seasoning salt

Combine all ingredients thoroughly in a baking dish. Bake at 350 degrees for 20 minutes.

DILLED & CHILLED CHEESE DIP

1 cup of cheddar cheese, shredded
4 teaspoons of horseradish
1 cup of sour cream
½ teaspoon of dill weed

Blend ingredients in a bowl. Cover and chill for 4 hours.

"DON'T BAKE 'EM" GRANOLA BARS

½ cup of corn syrup
½ cup of peanut butter
2 cups of granola cereal
¼ cup of raisins
¼ cup of peanuts (or nut of choice)

Combine granola, raisins and nuts and mix well. Heat corn syrup to a boil and blend in peanut butter. Immediately pour over granola mixture and mix quickly to coat. Press firmly into an 8-inch square pan. Cool before cutting into bars. Makes a dozen hefty bars for the deer blind of fishing boat.

EVERGREEN RICE DISH

5 green onions
½ green pepper, diced
4 stalks of celery
3 tablespoons of margarine or butter
1 cup of raw rice
1 cup of mushrooms (drained if canned)
4 tablespoons of parsley, chopped
2 cups chicken bouillon or stock

Sauté green onions, green pepper and celery in margarine. Stir in rice and add chicken bouillon. Cook covered for 20 to 30 minutes. For the last 10 minutes, add mushrooms and parsley and leave cover off. Put in casserole or baking dish to heat.

MACARONI SALAD

2 cups of cooked macaroni
1 cup of cheese, finely shredded
½ cup of stuffed olives, sliced (optional)
½ cup of celery, diced
1 small onion, diced
2 hard-boiled eggs, diced
Mayonnaise and salt

This one ain't brain surgery. Mix it together as you see fit.

MAC-CHICKEN NUGGETS

4 chicken breasts
1 cup of breadcrumbs
½ cup of Parmesan cheese
1 teaspoon of thyme
1 teaspoon of basil
½ teaspoon of salt
¾ cup of margarine or butter

Cut up chicken into nugget size. Melt margarine. Mix other ingredients together. Dip chicken into margarine then bread crumb mixture. Place on a cookie sheet and bake at 350 degrees for 45 minutes.

MOM'S HOMEMADE APPLESAUCE

8 apples peeled, cored and sliced
½ cup of water
½ cup of brown sugar
1 teaspoon of cinnamon

Heat apples and water in a deep pan for 5 to 10 minutes, stirring occasionally. Mix in the rest of the ingredients. Heat until it starts to boil and stir for 1 minute. For smaller parties cut the recipe in half.

ORANGE DREAM JELL-O SALAD

2 3-ounce packages of orange Jell-O
1 pint of orange sherbet
1 small can of mandarin oranges, drained
1½ cups of boiling water
1 cup of juice from mandarin oranges and
  water mixed
½ pint of whipping cream

Dissolve Jell-O in boiling water. Add sherbet immediately, stirring until dissolved. Add remaining liquid. Stir and chill until partially set. Whip cream and fold into Jell-O. Fold in mandarin oranges, pour into dish or mold. Chill until firm.

OVEN JERKY

5 pounds of venison or beef
1¾ cups of brown sugar
4 ounces of meat cure
3½ ounces of soy sauce
3 tablespoons of liquid smoke
4 cloves of garlic, minced

Cut meat into ¼ inch strips, removing fat. Combine ingredients in a Ziploc bag. Once mixed, put meat in bag and seal it. Place in fridge for 12 hours; knead every 2 to 3 hours. Remove meat from bag, wash and towel dry. Put on oven rack at low heat for 11 to 12 hours.

OVEN ROASTED POTATOES

2½ pounds of red potatoes
¼ cup of olive oil
2 teaspoons of salt
¼ teaspoon of paprika
½ teaspoon of pepper

Rinse, dry and chop potatoes into cubes. Combine oil, salt, paprika and pepper. Mix well. Add potatoes and toss. Place on an oiled tray. Bake at 425 degrees for 45 minutes until tender and well browned. Turn every 15 minutes.

POKER NIGHT CHICKEN WINGS

24 chicken wings
1 cup of pineapple juice
1 cup of soy sauce
1 cup of sugar
¼ cup of water
¼ cup of vegetable oil
2 cloves of garlic, crushed
1 teaspoon of ginger

Combine all ingredients in pan except chicken and ginger. Once thoroughly combined, add ginger and refrigerate overnight. Next day, pour off about 1 cup of liquid and place chicken in the pan. Bake uncovered at 350 degrees for 60 minutes. Baste wings with remaining liquid during baking.

POP JELL-O SALAD

6-ounce package of lemon or cherry Jell-O
1 cup of regular cola
1 cup of water
10 ounces of maraschino cherries,
    drained and chopped

Dissolve Jell-O into a cup of boiling water. Add coke and cherries. Put in a dish and refrigerate until firm. If you're a cherry fanatic, use Cherry Coke.

PORCUPINE MOUNTAIN MEATBALLS

1½ pounds of ground beef
½ cup of rice, washed
1 teaspoon of salt
½ teaspoon of pepper
1 tablespoon of onion, minced
1 can of tomato soup
½ cup of water

Combine beef, rice, salt, pepper and onion, shape into small balls. Heat tomato soup and ½ cup of water in a pan. Drop meatballs into soup mixture and cover. Simmer for one hour.

PETOSKEY POTATO SALAD

5 pounds of potatoes with skins,
  boiled & diced
1 pound of sharp cheddar cheese, cubed
1 large onion, diced
2 cups of mayonnaise
4 teaspoons of Dijon mustard
4 splashes of Tabasco sauce
4 strips of bacon
Salt to taste

Mix potatoes, cheese and onion. In a separate bowl mix mayo, mustard, Tabasco and salt. Combine the two mixtures and top with the bacon. Bake at 350 degrees for 1 hour.

SMOKED FISH SPREAD

1½ pounds of smoked fish
2 teaspoons of onion, minced
2 teaspoons of celery, finely diced
1 clove of garlic, minced
2 teaspoons of sweet pickles, finely diced
1¼ cups of mayonnaise or Miracle Whip
1 tablespoon of mustard
2 tablespoons of parsley, chopped
Dash of Worcestershire sauce

Remove skin and bones from fish then flake well. Mix all ingredients and chill for 2 hours. Serve with crackers.

STUFFED JALAPENOS

¼ pound of ground beef
12 popper-size jalapeños
1 small onion
1 pound of bacon
14 ounces Monterey Jack with jalapeños
Oil

Chop onion and brown in oil. Add hamburger, brown and drain. Grate cheese and mix with hamburger. Cut top of jalapeños and core out the seeds. Slit down to ¼ inch from bottom. Stuff jalapenos with the hamburger mixture. Wrap slice of bacon around popper. Stick with toothpick if needed. Bake, broil or grill.

SUPERIOR SHORES WILD RICE

1 cup of wild rice, thoroughly rinsed
1 cup of chicken soup
3 cups of water
¼ cup of celery
¼ cup of onions
¼ cup of mushrooms
2 tablespoons of almond slivers (optional)
2 tablespoons of margarine or butter

Cook rice in water for 45 to 55 minutes in a covered pot. Sauté remaining ingredients together in a separate pan. When rice is tender add in the sautéed ingredients and stir.

TWO-STEP SALAD DRESSING

¾ cup Miracle Whip or Mayonnaise
¼ cup ketchup

Whip together. Diced sweet pickle or relish can be stirred in too but is optional. For a richer flavor mix ingredients in a 1:1 ratio.

WOODS & WATER JERKY SNACK

Jerky (of choice)
Unsalted, roasted peanuts
Cashews
Raisins
Dates, chopped
Sunflower seeds
M&M's or Reese's Pieces
Dried bananas

Cut jerky into small bits and add equal amounts of other ingredients. Works better in the fishing boat. The scent and crunching disturbs the deer.

DESSERTS

APPLE CAKE

2 eggs, slightly beaten
10 tablespoons of melted butter
2 teaspoons of vanilla
2 cups of flour
2 cups of sugar
3 cups of chopped apples
1 cup of chopped nuts (optional)
1 cup of raisins

Mix eggs, butter and vanilla. Add dry ingredients that have been sifted together. Then add apples, nuts and raisins. Bake at 350 degrees for 30 to 35 minutes.

APPLE CRISP

5 Granny Smith apples, sliced
½ cup of sugar
½ cup of flour
½ cup of uncooked quick-cooking oats
¾ cup of brown sugar
1 ounce of lemon juice
8 ounces of soft margarine and butter

Combine apples, sugar and lemon juice. Arrange in a 12-inch by 9-inch baking dish. Combine remaining ingredients and mix until crumbly. Spread evenly over apples. Bake at 350 degrees 45 to 50 minutes.

BLUEBERRY BARS

1 cup of flour
½ teaspoon of salt
2½ cups of fresh blueberries
1 cup of oatmeal
½ cup of shortening (Crisco)
½ cup of granulated sugar

Mix flour, oatmeal, salt and shortening together thoroughly. Spread half of the mixture into a greased 8-inch by 8-inch pan. Mix blueberries with sugar and spread them over the flour mixture in the pan. Cover the blueberries with the remaining half of the flour mixture. Press lightly. Bake at 375 degrees for 40 to 45 minutes. Cut when cool.

CAMP COOKIES

2 sticks of butter
4 cups of sugar
1 cup of milk
6 tablespoons of cocoa
6 cups of oats
1 cup of crunchy peanut butter
2 tablespoons of vanilla

Mix butter, sugar, milk and cocoa and bring to a rolling boil for one minute. Add remaining ingredients, mix well and pour into a buttered pan.

CHEESE CAKE

4 eggs
1 cup of sugar
1 cup of sour cream
1 large piecrust
8 ounces of cream cheese
1 teaspoon of vanilla extract
Juice from 1 lemon

Mix eggs, sugar, sour cream, vanilla and lemon juice thoroughly. Use a blender if handy. Pour into piecrust. Bake at 350 degrees for 30 minutes.

CHOCOLATE BROWNIES

1 cup of margarine or butter
3 squares of chocolate
1 tablespoon of cocoa
2¼ cups of sugar
5 eggs
2 teaspoons of vanilla
1¾ cups of flour
1 teaspoon of salt

Melt margarine, chocolate and cocoa then let cool. Add remaining ingredients. Pour into a 9" x 13" pan and bake at 350 degrees fro 30 to 35 minutes. Frost if you prefer. Nuts can be included in the batter or sprinkled on top.

CITRUS SUGAR COOKIES

1 cup of margarine or butter
3 cups of flour
1 cup of sugar
1 egg, beaten
1 teaspoon of lemon or orange zest
½ teaspoon lemon or orange juice
½ teaspoon salt

First, pick lemon or orange flavor. Mix ingredients thoroughly. Refrigerate overnight or at least 2 hours. Roll mixture on a floured surface. Cut into shapes. Bake on un-greased cookie sheet at 375 degrees for 8 to 10 minutes.

FRIDGE-BAKED CHOCOLATE PIE

20 regular-sized marshmallows
2/3 cup of milk
1 8-inch graham cracker piecrust
4 small Hershey chocolate bars
1 cup of whipped cream

Combine chocolate bars, milk and marshmallows in a double boiler or similar set-up until melted. Water should not be hot but not boiling. Let mixture cool then fold in whipped cream and pour into piecrust. Refrigerate.

HOMEMADE ICE CREANM

6 eggs
6 cups of milk
4 cups of Half & Half
2½ cups of sugar
2 tablespoons of vanilla extract
1 pinch of salt

Beat eggs until fluffy. Add sugar slowly and beat until fluffy. Pour into freezer. Add salt, Half & Half and vanilla. Mix. Fill to within 1 inch of top. For chocolate ice cream: add 1 can of Hershey's chocolate syrup and subtract an equal amount of milk.

LAKE GOGEBIC COOKIES

1 cup of Crisco
1 cup of butter
1 cup of sugar
1 cup of brown sugar
2 eggs
2 teaspoons of vanilla
2 cups of flour
1 teaspoon of baking powder
1 teaspoon of soda
1 cup of coconut
2 cups of Rice Krispies
2 cups of oatmeal
Pinch of salt

Mix all the ingredients thoroughly. Drop teaspoons of the mixture onto a cookie sheet. Bake at 350 degrees for 10 minutes.

SALVATION ARMY DOUGHNUTS

5 cups of flour
2 cups of sugar
½ teaspoon of salt
1 teaspoon of nutmeg
2 eggs
5 teaspoons of baking powder
1¼ cups of milk
1 teaspoon melted butter

Sift dry ingredients. Combine eggs, butter and milk. Add dry ingredients. Mix well. Shape into a ball and knead. Roll out on floured surface and cut with doughnut cutter. Place in deep fryer or in a deep skillet. Makes four dozen. This recipe was used to serve tens of thousands of allied troops throughout Europe during World War I.

SUGAR COOKIES

1 cup of margarine
1 cup of sugar
1 teaspoon of cream of tartar
1 teaspoon of vanilla or almond extract
1 cup of powdered sugar
2 eggs
1 teaspoon of baking soda
4 cups of flour

Cream margarine and sugar, and then add remaining ingredients. Drop on cookie sheet and flatten slightly with the bottom of a wet glass dipped in sugar. Bake at 350 degrees for 8 to 10 minutes.

WHEATIES COOKIES

1 cup of shortening
1 cup of white sugar
1 cup of brown sugar
2 eggs
2¼ cups of flour
1 teaspoon of baking soda
1 cup of coconut
1 teaspoon of baking powder
2 cups of Wheaties
2 teaspoons of vanilla

Cream shortening, sugars and eggs together. Sift and add all dry ingredients. Add vanilla then add Wheaties and coconut. Form into a ball a little smaller than a golf ball. Bake at 325 degrees for 15 to 20 minutes or until light brown.

WINE COUNTRY CAKE

1 package of white or yellow cake mix
¾ cup of sherry wine
¾ cup of oil
4 eggs
¼ teaspoon of nutmeg
1 package of vanilla or butterscotch pudding
(not instant)

Grease and flour two loaf pans. Put all ingredients in bowl. Beat for 8 minutes. Pour into loaf pans and bake at 350 degrees for 60 minutes.

WORLD'S EASIEST COOKIE

Guys, even you can pull this one off. It's three ingredients, but don't burn the chips! Keep the heat low.

> 6 ounces of butterscotch chips
> 12 ounces of chocolate chips
> 1 large package of chow mien noodles

Melt chips together and stir in noodles thoroughly. Drop spoonfuls of the cookie batter onto wax paper with a spoon and let cool.

BREADS & BISCUITS

BEER BREAD

3 cups of self-rising flour
3 tablespoons of sugar
1 can of beer
3 tablespoons of melted butter

Combine ingredients thoroughly and pour into a greased loaf pan. Bake at 350 degrees for 45 minutes or until golden brown. Brush/drizzle melted butter on top.

BEER MUFFINS

2 cups of Bisquick
2 tablespoons of sugar
1 cup of beer
1 cup of cheddar cheese, shredded

Mix all the ingredients and fill greased muffin cup 2/3 full with the batter. Let stand for 12 minutes and bake at 375 degrees for 15 minutes. Makes 12 muffins.

BACON CHEDDAR CORN BREAD

If you have ever doubted the existence of God, one taste of these (when made properly) will re-affirm your faith in a higher being.

>   1 cup of flour
>   ¼ cup of sugar
>   2 teaspoons of baking powder
>   1 teaspoon of baking soda
>   ½ teaspoon of salt
>   1¼ cups of yellow corn meal
>   1½ cups of low-fat or regular buttermilk
>   1 large egg
>   1 cup sharp cheddar cheese, grated
>   4 thick slices of cooked bacon, shredded
>   2 tablespoons unsalted butter, melted
>   (plus softened butter for greasing pan)

Sift flour, sugar, baking powder, baking soda and salt into a bowl. Add cornmeal and mix well. Mix buttermilk, egg and butter in a separate bowl. Pour flour mixture over buttermilk mixture and stir slowly until combined. Add bacon and cheese and stir. Pour into a lightly greased 9-inch pan and bake at 400 degrees for about 20 minutes.

BASIC BISCUITS

2 cups of flour (and a little for kneading)
½ cup of shortening
1 teaspoon of salt
3 teaspoons of baking powder
1 cup of milk (buttermilk optional)

Mix flour and shortening until pieces are the size of marbles or a little smaller. Add salt and baking powder. Also add baking soda only if you used buttermilk. Knead briefly on a floured surface. Roll out to 1 inch thick and cut. Put on a greased baking sheet. Don't let the biscuits touch. Bake at 400 degrees just until the edges are golden brown.

BUTTERSCOTCH ROLLS

2 loaves of frozen bread dough
1 box of butterscotch pudding mix
1 cup of brown sugar
½ cup of milk
½ cup of melted butter
1 teaspoon of cinnamon
1 teaspoon of vanilla

Thaw bread dough and cut into cubes. Place the bread in a 9-inch by 13-inch pan or Bundt pan. Mix remaining ingredients and pour over bread cubes. Let rise until it doubles in size. Bake at 350 degrees for 30 minutes.

CORNBREAD

2 cups of corn meal
1 cup of white flour
4 teaspoons of baking powder
2 teaspoons of salt
1 cup of sugar
4 tablespoons of melted butter
2 eggs
1 cup of milk
4 tablespoons of honey

Mix corn meal, flour, baking powder and salt. Add sugar and melted butter. Beat eggs and add to mixture along with milk. Pour into a greased 9-inch by 13-inch pan and bake at 350 degrees for 20 to 25 minutes until top of bread is light brown. Spread thin glaze of honey on top and return it to the oven for 10 more minutes.

D.I.Y. BREAD STICKS

Hot dog buns
Melted butter
Crushed garlic
Parmesan cheese
Sesame seeds, browned (optional)

Split buns in quarters. Brush with melted butter and add crushed garlic clove. Roll in Parmesan cheese and browned sesame seeds. Toast carefully.

HOBO BREAD

2 cups of raisins
2 teaspoons of baking soda
1 cup of sugar
1 egg
¼ cup of salad oil
½ teaspoon of salt
2 teaspoons of baking powder
2½ cups of flour
1 cup of nuts (optional)

Put raisins and baking soda in a bowl, add 2 cups of boiling water and let soak overnight. In the morning, add remaining ingredients and mix well. Put mixture into 2 greased loaf pans. Place pans in a larger rimmed pan with 1-inch of water and bake at 350 degrees for 40 to 45 minutes.

BEVERAGES

CITRUS CIDER

    2 quarts of pure apple cider
    2 quarts of grapefruit juice
       (fresh squeezed if possible)

Combine chilled juices and mix thoroughly. Alcohol may be added.

DEER CAMP HOLIDAY PUNCH

2 cans of frozen orange juice
2 cans of frozen lemonade
2 cups of grenadine
3 quarts of cold ginger ale
8 cans of water (frozen juice cans)
Orange slices
Cherries

Mix the liquids. Float orange slices on top and add cherries. Makes approximately 1½ gallons.

EGG NOG

2 eggs
2 tablespoons of sugar
2 teaspoons of vanilla
2 cups of milk

Mix egg sugar, vanilla and 2/3 cup milk in blender. Mix at high speed for one minute. Add remaining milk and mix well until blended.

FIRESIDE COFFEE

1 cup of hot chocolate powder mix
1 cup of non-dairy creamer
½ cup of instant coffee
½ teaspoon of cinnamon
¼ teaspoon of nutmeg
½ to ¾ cup sugar (adjust to taste)

Mix hot chocolate, creamer, coffee, cinnamon and nutmeg in a blender. Add in sugar and blend well. Drop in 3 to 4 heaping teaspoons per mug and pour in hot water.

HOLIDAY CIDER

1½ cups of sugar
3 cups of water
3 cinnamon sticks
4 whole cloves
1 cup of orange juice
4 cups of apple juice or cider
1 cup of lemon juice
2 cups of pineapple juice
2 quarts of water

Simmer sugar, water, cinnamon and cloves for 30 minutes. Add in remaining ingredients. Heat and stir, but do not boil.

PINK LEMONADE MILK SHAKE

1½ cups of frozen pink lemonade
    concentrate
3 cups of milk
10 scoops of vanilla ice cream

Mix all ingredients thoroughly in a blender. Makes five to six servings. Works with regular lemonade too.

HOME-BREWED ROOT BEER

2 cups of sugar
½ bottle of root beer extract
1 teaspoon of dry yeast
½ cup of warm water
1 to 2 cups of water

Pour 3 tablespoons or ½ bottle of root beer extract over 2 cups sugar and add enough water to dissolve. Add 1 teaspoon of dry yeast to ½ cup warm water to dissolve. Add both mixtures together and pour into gallon jug. Top of jug with warm water and let set for 6 hours uncapped. Tighten lid and refrigerate. After 24 hours it's ready to drink. The longer it sets, the better it tastes.

OLD FASHIONED LEMONADE

6 lemons (or 1 cup of the bottled stuff)
6 cups of cold water
1 cup of sugar

Juice lemons until you have 1 cup of fresh lemon juice. Mix the fresh juice with water and sugar in a pitcher. Stir and pour over ice.

FAUX ORANGE JULIUS

6-ounce can of frozen orange juice
1 cup of water
1 egg
12 ice cubes
1 cup of milk (whole or 2%)
½ cup of sugar
1 teaspoon of vanilla

Put all ingredients in blender and whip for 15 seconds.

QUICK PUNCH

3 quarts of 7-Up or lemon lime soda
6 ounces of fresh lemon juice
6-ounce can of frozen orange juice
6-ounce can of frozen lemonade

Mix in a bowl or pot, adding the soda last. Stir in ice. Makes almost a gallon.

Made in the USA
San Bernardino, CA
24 November 2014